OXFORD FREE LIBRARY
339 MAIN ST.
OXFORD, MA 01540

Melting Ice

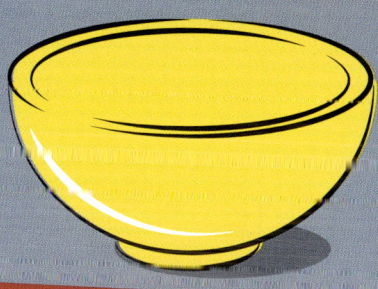

my science fun

Published in the United States of America by Cherry Lake Publishing
Ann Arbor, Michigan
www.cherrylakepublishing.com

Reading Adviser: Marla Conn MS, Ed., Literacy specialist, Read-Ability, Inc.
Book Design: Jennifer Wahi
Illustrator: Jeff Bane

Copyright ©2018 by Cherry Lake Publishing
All rights reserved. No part of this book may be reproduced or utilized in any form or by any means without written permission from the publisher.

Library of Congress Cataloging-in-Publication Data has been filed and is available at catalog.loc.gov

Printed in the United States of America
Corporate Graphics

About the illustrator: Jeff Bane and his two business partners own a studio along the American River in Folsom, California, home of the 1849 Gold Rush. When Jeff's not sketching or illustrating for clients, he's either swimming or kayaking in the river to relax.

table of contents

Asking Questions 4

Science Fun 8

Glossary & Index 24

Science Notes

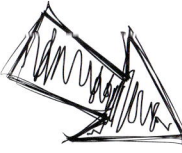 *Melting Ice* explores how ice turns to liquid water faster when salt is sprinkled on it. In this experiment, the reader sprinkles salt in one bowl of ice and compares it to another bowl of ice without salt. The salt lowers the freezing point of the ice, creating holes and channels in the ice cubes. This speeds up the melting.

asking questions

Ice is frozen water.

Streets can have ice. It's unsafe for cars. Workers help melt the ice.

Do you drink water with ice? Why?

How can you make ice melt?

Let's find out!

science fun

- Ice cubes
- 2 bowls
- Camera
- **Salt**

You will need these things

Fill both bowls with the same amount of ice. Take a picture of them.

Add salt in one bowl of ice.
Leave the other bowl alone.
Take a picture of them.

Wait 10 minutes. Take another picture.

Review your three photos.
Look at how the ice changed.

Why is it helpful to take photos?

The ice with salt melted faster.

Try it with different types of salt.

Good job. You're done!
Science is fun!

What new questions do you have?

glossary & index

glossary

review (rih-VYOO) to study or go over something

salt (SAWLT) a white substance used to add flavor to foods

index

faster, 18
frozen, 4, 21

melt, 4, 6, 18

photos, 16-17

water, 4-5